DNA

Dennis Kelly is an internationally acclaimed writer with his plays performed in over thirty countries. Stage plays include *Debris* (Theatre503/Battersea Arts Centre, 2003), *Osama the Hero* (Hampstead Theatre, 2004), *After the End* (Paines Plough, Traverse Theatre, Bush Theatre, 2005), *Love and Money* (Young Vic/Manchester Royal Exchange, 2006), *Taking Care of Baby* (Hampstead Theatre/Birmingham Repertory, 2006), *DNA* (National Theatre, 2008), *Orphans* (Paines Plough, Traverse Theatre, Soho Theatre & Birmingham Rep, 2009), *The Gods Weep* (Royal Shakespeare Company, 2010) and *The Ritual Slaughter of Gorge Mastromas* (Frankfurt Schauspielhaus, 2011). For Television he co-wrote and created *Pulling* (Silver River/BBC Three) and has written and created *Utopia* (Kudos) for Channel Four. He also wrote the book for *Matilda the Musical* (Royal Shakespeare Company).

Anthony Banks is from Manchester and studied English at King's College London before training as a director at the Royal Academy of Dramatic Art. He is Associate Director for National Theatre Learning, where he commissions and develops scripts for the NT Connections seasons and Primary Theatre programme and curates a variety of projects and events for lifelong learning.

His directing includes: Bryony Lavery's *More Light*, Lucinda Coxon's *The Eternal Not* and Michael Lesslie's *Prince of Denmark* (National Theatre); Calderón's *El Gran Teatro Del Mundo* (Royal Festival Hall); Snoo Wilson's *Pignight* (Menier Chocolate Factory); Doug Lucie's *Shellshock* (BBC); Mark Ravenhill's *The Experiment* (Soho Theatre & Berliner Ensemble); Lucinda Coxon's *Herding Cats* (Theatre Royal Bath & Hampstead Theatre); James Graham's *Bassett* (Bristol Old Vic); Dennis Kelly's *DNA* (National Tour); Tosin Omosebi's *ReWrite* (Westminster Hall and National Theatre); Bryony Lavery's *Cesario* (World Shakespeare Festival, National Theatre and Tate Modern); Tennessee Williams' *The Hotel Plays* (Grange Holborn).

Dennis Kelly

DNA

School Edition

with notes for teachers and students

by Anthony Banks

OBERON BOOKS
LONDON

DNA (original version) first published in 2008
by Oberon Books Ltd
521 Caledonian Road, London N7 9RH
Tel: +44 (0) 20 7607 3637 / Fax: +44 (0) 20 7607 3629
e-mail: info@oberonbooks.com
www.oberonbooks.com

School Edition first published in 2009

Reprinted in 2010 (twice), 2011 (thrice), 2012, 2013, 2014 (twice), 2015 (twice), 2016, 2017

Cover photograph: stock.xchng (www.sxc.hu)

Printed and bound by Replika Press Pvt. Ltd., India.

Visit www.oberonbooks.com to read more about all our books and to buy them. You will also find features, author interviews and news of any author events, and you can sign up for e-newsletters so that you're always first to hear about our new releases.

Contents

Characters

MARK and JAN,

LEAH and PHIL,

LOU, JOHN TATE and DANNY,

RICHARD,

CATHY and BRIAN, and

a BOY.

Takes place in a Street, a Field and a Wood.

Names and genders of characters are suggestions only,
and can be changed to suit performers.

DNA was first performed in the Cottesloe Theatre of the National Theatre, on 16 February 2008, with the following Company:

MARK, Gregg Chillin

JAN, Claire Foy

LEAH, Ruby Bentall

PHIL, Sam Crane

JOHN TATE, Jack Gordon

DANNY, Benjamin Smith

RICHARD, Troy Glasgow

CATHY, Claire Lams

BRIAN, Ian Bonar

BOY, Ryan Sampson

All other parts played by members of the Company.

Director Paul Miller

Designer Simon Daw

Lighting Designer Paule Constable

Sound Designer Rich Walsh

Associate Video Designer Paul Kenah

This play was commissioned by National Theatre Education as part of its Connections project.

One

A Street. MARK and JAN.

JAN: Dead?

MARK: Yeah.

JAN: What, dead?

MARK: Yeah

JAN: Like dead, dead

MARK: Yes

JAN: proper dead, not living dead?

MARK: Not living dead, yes.

JAN: Are you sure?

MARK: Yes.

JAN: I mean there's no

MARK: No.

JAN: mistake or

MARK: No mistake.

JAN: it's not a joke

MARK: It's not a joke.

JAN: coz it's not funny.

MARK: it's not funny because it's not a joke, if it was a joke it
would be funny.

JAN: Not hiding?

MARK: Not hiding, dead.

JAN: not

MARK: Dead.

JAN: Oh.

MARK: Yes.

JAN: God.

MARK: Yes.

JAN: God.

MARK: Exactly.

Pause.

JAN: What are we going to do?

*   *   *

A Field. LEAH and PHIL, PHIL eating an ice cream.

LEAH: What are you thinking?

No answer.

No, don't tell me, sorry, that's a stupid, that's such a stupid –

You can tell me, you know. You can talk to me. I won't judge you, whatever it is. Whatever you're, you know, I won't, I won't…

Is it me?

Not that I'm –

I mean it wouldn't matter if you weren't or were, actually, so –

Are you thinking about me?

No answer.

What good things? Phil? Or…

I mean is it a negative, are you thinking a negative thing about –

Not that I'm bothered. I'm not bothered, Phil, I'm not, it doesn't, I don't care. You know. I don't...

What, like I talk too much? Is that it? That I talk too much, you, sitting there in absolute silence thinking 'Leah talks too much, I wish she'd shut up once in a while' is that it, is that what you're, because don't, you know, judge, you know, because alright, I do. There, I'm admitting, I am admitting, I talk too much, so shoot me. So kill me, Phil, call the police, lock me up, rip out my teeth with a pair of rusty pliers, I talk too much, what a crime, what a sin, what an absolute catastrophe, stupid, evil, ridiculous, because you're not perfect actually, Phil. Okay? There. I've said it, you're not...

You're a bit...

You're...

Pause. She sits.

Do I disgust you? I do. No, I do. No don't because, it's alright, it's fine, I'm not gonna, you know, or whatever, you know it's not the collapse of my, because I do have, I could walk out of here, there are friends, I've got, I've got friends, I mean alright, I haven't got friends, not exactly, I haven't, but I could, if I wanted, if I wanted, given the right, given the perfect, you know, circumstances. So don't, because you haven't either, I mean it's not like you're, you know, Mr, you know, popular, you know, you haven't, you know, you haven't, you know, you haven't, but that's, that's different, isn't it, I mean it is, it is, don't say it isn't, really, don't, you'll just embarrass us both because it is different, it's different because it doesn't matter to you. Does it. Sitting there. Sitting there, all...

all...

You're not scared. Nothing scares, there, I've said it; scared. Scared, Phil. I'm scared, they scare me, this place, everyone, the fear, the fear that everyone here, and I'm not the only one, I'm not the only one, Phil, I'm just the only one saying it, the fear that everyone here lives in, the brutal terror, it scares me, okay, I've said it and I am not ashamed. Yes, I am ashamed but I'm not ashamed of my shame, Phil, give me that much credit at least, thank you.

Everyone's scared.

S'not just me.

Pause.

We've got each other.

We need each other.

So don't give it all…

You need me as much as…

Don't give it all the…

Beat.

What are you thinking?

JAN and MARK enter.

Pause.

MARK: We need to talk to you.

LEAH: Oh, shit.

*   *   *

A wood. LOU, JOHN TATE and DANNY.

LOU: Screwed.

JOHN TATE: No, no, it's not, no, Lou, we're not

LOU: We are screwed.

JOHN TATE: No, Lou, we're not…it's not…we're not…
nothing's….

LOU: It is.

JOHN TATE: No, no, no, look, there I have to, I really have to,
you're going to have to listen to me on this one, and you
are going to have to believe me. Everything is, everything's
fine.

LOU: Fine?

JOHN TATE: Not fine, no

DANNY: Fine?

JOHN TATE: not fine exactly, alright, fair enough, I mean
things are bad, things are a little, alright, yes, I'm not trying
to hide the, this is tricky, it's a tricky

LOU: Tricky?

JOHN TATE: situation, but it's not, because actually what you
are saying is a very negative, and that's…

Look, haven't I looked after things before?

LOU: This is different.

JOHN TATE: Lou, are you scared of anyone in this school?

LOU: You?

JOHN TATE: Apart from me.

LOU: No.

JOHN TATE: Exactly

LOU: Richard, maybe

JOHN TATE: exactly, that's exactly, that's what I'm saying –
Richard, you're scared of, are you…? – I mean you can
walk down any corridor in this – I don't think Richard's –
any corridor in this school and you know, no one bothers
you and if you want something it's yours and no one

bothers you and everyone respects you and everyone's scared of you and who made that, I mean I'm not boasting, but who made that happen?

LOU: You.

JOHN TATE: Thank you, so are things really that bad?

LOU: Yes.

JOHN TATE: Richard? I mean are you really?

DANNY: I can't get mixed up in this. I'm gonna be a dentist.

LOU: This is different, John. This is

JOHN TATE: Alright, it's a little bit

LOU: This is really serious.

DANNY: Dentists don't get mixed up in things. I've got a plan. I've got a plan John, I've made plans, and this is not...

JOHN TATE: It's a bit serious, but let's not, I mean come on, let's not over play the, the, the

LOU: He's dead.

JOHN TATE: the gravity of… Well, yes, okay, fair enough, but

DANNY: This is not part of the plan. Dental college is part of the plan, A-levels are part of the plan, dead people are not part of the plan, this is not Dental college.

LOU: He's dead, John.

JOHN TATE: Alright, I'm not denying, am I denying? no, I'm

LOU: He's dead.

JOHN TATE: Well, don't keep saying it.

DANNY: This is the opposite of Dental college.

LOU: But he is dead.

JOHN TATE: Well you just, you're saying it again, didn't I just –

LOU: Because he's dead, John, he's dead, dead is what he is so we have to use that word to –

JOHN TATE: Alright. New rule; that word is banned.

Beat.

LOU: What, 'dead'?

JOHN TATE: Yes.

DANNY: Banned?

JOHN TATE: Yes. Banned. Sorry.

LOU: You can't ban a word.

JOHN TATE: and if anyone says it I'm going to have to, you know, bite their face. Or something.

DANNY: How can you ban a word?

JOHN TATE: Well just say it then.

Pause.

Say it and see what happens.

They say nothing.

Look, we have to keep together. We have to trust each other and believe in each other. I'm trying to help. I'm trying to keep things together.

RICHARD enters, with CATHY and BRIAN, CATHY grinning, BRIAN crying.

Pause.

RICHARD: He's dead.

JOHN TATE: Right, that's…now I really am getting a little bit cross, do not use that word.

RICHARD: What?

JOHN TATE: No one says that word, okay, no one.

RICHARD: What, word?

CATHY: This is mad, eh?

JOHN TATE: You know.

CATHY: Talk about mad. I mean, it's quite exciting as well, though, isn't it.

RICHARD: What, 'dead'?

JOHN TATE: Don't say it again, Richard, or I'm gonna

CATHY: Better than ordinary life.

RICHARD: What?

JOHN TATE: I'm gonna

RICHARD: What?

JOHN TATE: I'm gonna

I'm gonna hurt you, actually.

Beat.

RICHARD: You're going to hurt me?

JOHN TATE: Yes.

RICHARD: Me?

JOHN TATE: Yes. If you use that word.

CATHY: I mean I'm not saying it's a good thing, but in a way it is.

DANNY: Shut up, Cathy.

CATHY: You shut up.

JOHN TATE: I am trying to keep everyone together. Ever since I came to this school haven't I been trying to keep everyone together? Aren't things better? For us? I mean not for them, not out there, but for us? Doesn't everyone

want to be us, come here in the woods? Isn't that worth
keeping hold of?

They say nothing. RICHARD steps forward, a little hesitantly.

RICHARD: You shouldn't threaten me, John.

JOHN TATE: I beg your pardon.

RICHARD: I'm just saying. I'm just saying, I've just walked
in here. I've been with these two. I've walked all the way
from school with these two, with him crying and with her
being weird, and I've just walked in here and I've got you
threatening me, you shouldn't threaten me, you shouldn't
threaten me, John.

Pause.

JOHN TATE: Or what?

RICHARD: What?

JOHN TATE: No, I mean, you know, or what?

RICHARD: Well…

JOHN TATE: Because I'm interested.

DANNY: He's just saying, John.

JOHN TATE: Are you on his side, Danny?

DANNY: No, I'm just saying that he's just saying.

CATHY: Shut up, Danny.

DANNY: You shut up.

JOHN TATE: Don't tell Cathy to shut up, Danny, that's really,
not…

DANNY: I'm not telling her to –

CATHY: He's on Richard's side.

DANNY: I'm not!

JOHN TATE: Are you, Danny? Are you on Richard's side?

DANNY: No –

CATHY: He is.

RICHARD: What do you mean by my side, there is no –

JOHN TATE: Have you got a side now, Richard?

RICHARD: No, no, there's no –

JOHN TATE: because that's a bit, is that what you've got?

DANNY: John, I'm not on –

JOHN TATE: Because if you've got a side that means you're not on my side and if you're not on my side that means you're setting yourself up against me and I thought we'd got over all that silliness.

RICHARD: We have, we –

JOHN TATE: I thought we were mates now.

RICHARD: We are, we are mates now, we –

JOHN TATE: So if me and Richard are mates now, which we are and all that silliness is over, which it is, and you're on someone's side, Danny, then you're on your own side, which is very, well, to be honest, very silly and dangerous.

DANNY: No, you've got it wrong, that's not –

JOHN TATE: Are you on my side?

DANNY: Yes, I'm on your side!

JOHN TATE: Which means you want...?

DANNY: I want to keep calm, I want to say nothing, just like you, you're right, you're right, John.

JOHN TATE: So what are you on about, Cathy?

CATHY: I'm –

JOHN TATE: Are you on my side? With Richard and Danny? Are you on our side, Cathy?

CATHY: Yes.

JOHN TATE: Good. Lou?

LOU: Yes.

JOHN TATE: You're on our side, Lou?

LOU: Yes, John.

JOHN TATE: You sure?

LOU: Yeah, I'm –

JOHN TATE: That just leaves you, Brian. You crying little piece of filth.

Beat. BRIAN stops crying. Looks up.

BRIAN: I think we should tell someone.

JOHN TATE begins to walk towards BRIAN.

MARK and JAN enter with LEAH and PHIL, PHIL drinking a Coke.

JOHN TATE stops.

Goes back to where he was.

JOHN TATE: I'm finding this all quite stressful. You know that? I'm under a lot of stress. You lot shouldn't put me under so much stress.

LEAH walks forward.

LEAH: Can I just say John, that we haven't done anything. First I want to say that, but if we have, John, but if we have done a thing, which we haven't, but if we have then we did it together. Whatever we did, we did, me and Phil, it wasn't just Phil, if that's what you're thinking, if you're thinking it might just have been him, on his own, without me, well that's not, we are completely, I am responsible as much as he, as much as Phil, but we didn't because –

JOHN TATE places a finger on her lips. She is silent.

JOHN TATE: Have you told them?

MARK: No.

JOHN TATE: Brilliant. Is there one thing that I do not have to do?

Beat.

JAN: So you want us to tell them?

JOHN TATE: Yes! Please.

He takes his finger away from LEAH's lips.

MARK: It's Adam. He's…

I mean we were just having a laugh, weren't we, we were all, you know…

You know Adam, you know what he's like, so we were sort of, well, alright, taking the piss, sort of. You know what he's like he was, sort of hanging around

JAN: Trying to be part of

MARK: Yeah, trying to be part of, yeah, yeah, so we're having a laugh

JAN: with him

MARK: yeah, with him, I mean he's laughing as well, see how far he'll go… We got him to eat some leaves.

JAN: Great big ones, dirty leaves off the floor, he ate them, just like that

MARK: Just like that, we were all

JAN: stitches

MARK: We were in stitches, weren't we

JAN: Adam too, he was

MARK: Oh yeah, Adam was, he was laughing harder than anyone.

JAN: Nutter.

MARK: Nutter.

JAN: complete

MARK: complete nutter

JAN: Big fist fulls of leaves, eh John

MARK: laughing his head off, eh John

JAN: He burnt his own socks!

MARK: Yeah, yeah, he did, that's right he, he set them alight

JAN: anything, he'd do, just a laugh

MARK: we got him to nick some vodka

JAN: you could tell he was scared

MARK: oh, he was terrified, he was completely, but like you know, pretending, you know, pretending he's done it before, big man, pretending he's

JAN: You know what he's like, he's

MARK: Do anything. And you're thinking 'Will he do anything? What won't he do?'

JAN: Let us punch him.

MARK: he was laughing

JAN: In the face.

MARK: He was laughing.

JAN: at first

MARK: Yeah, at first he was, I mean we took it a bit far, alright, half hour, forty minutes

JAN: I mean he was still joking all the way, but

MARK: you could tell

JAN: He weren't really

MARK: fear

JAN: well

MARK: you don't want to admit, you know what he's like, Phil…

JAN: Stubbed out cigarettes on him.

MARK: joking, we were

JAN: Arms, hands, face

MARK: having a laugh, really, he was laughing

JAN: and crying, soles of his feet

MARK: or crying, sort of, a bit of both

JAN: Made him run across the motorway

MARK: you're thinking what is this nutter, and with the vodka making you feel a bit, you know, you're having a laugh, together, what is this nutter gonna do next, we can make him do, we can make him do –

JAN: That's when I went home

MARK: anything, yeah, only because you had to.

JAN: I wasn't there when –

MARK: Only because you had to, you would've been there otherwise, you did all the…

Beat.

We went up the grille. You know, that shaft up there on the hill. Just a big hole really, hole with a grille over it, covering, just to see if he'd climb the fence, really and he did, and we thought, you know, he's climbed the fence which we didn't think he'd do so walk, you know, walk on the grille, Adam, walk on the, and he did, he's walked on, you know, wobbling and that but he's walking on the grille and we're all laughing and he's scared because if you slip, I mean it's just blackness under you, I mean it's only about fifteen foot wide so, but it might be hundreds of feet into blackness, I dunno, but he's doing it, he's walked on the grille. He's on the grille. He is.

And someone's pegged a stone at him.

Not to hit him, just for the laugh.

And you shoulda seen his face, I mean the fear, the, it was so, you had to laugh, the expression, the fear…

So we're all peggin them. Laughing. And his face, it's just making you laugh harder and harder, and they're getting nearer and nearer. And one hits his head. And the shock on his face is so…funny. And we're all just…

just…

really chucking these stones into him, really hard and laughing and he slips.

And he drops.

Into…

Into the er…

So he's…

So he's…

So he's –

JOHN TATE: Dead. He's dead.

Cathy says you're clever.

So. What do we do?

Pause. They all stare at LEAH and PHIL.

LEAH goes to say something, but nothing comes out.

Silence.

More silence.

PHIL puts his Coke carefully on the ground.

PHIL: Cathy, Danny, Mark, you go to Adam's house, you wait until his mum's out, you break in

DANNY: What?

PHIL: through an upstairs window so it's out of the way, make sure no one sees you. Get in, go to his bedroom, find a pair of his shoes and an item of his clothing, a jumper or something, don't touch the jumper, that's very important, do not touch the jumper, but you have to get it in the plastic bag without touching it

CATHY: What plastic bag?

PHIL: The refuse sacks that you are going to buy on the way, do not use the first one on the roll, use the third or fourth, do not be tempted to use a bin liner you have knocking around the house as that will be a DNA nightmare.

Richard, you take Brian to the Head, tell him that you found Brian crying in the toilets, asked him what was wrong and when he told you, you brought him here.

RICHARD: Me? But I hate him!

PHIL: Brian, you cry

RICHARD: Me with Brian?

PHIL: and you tell them a man showed you his willy in the woods

BRIAN: Wha…what?

PHIL: by the bridge, last week, a fat Caucasian male, 5'9" say, with thinning hair and a postman's uniform, sad eyes, softly spoken

DANNY: Who's that?

PHIL: The man who showed Brian his willy in the woods, please keep up, I'm making this up as I go along

DANNY: What were his teeth like?

PHIL: Bad, very bad.

DANNY: Thought so.

PHIL: Lou, Danny and Jan you take the shoes, Lou you put them on, and you enter the woods from the south entrance

CATHY: Which one's south?

MARK: By the Asda.

PHIL: Danny you enter from the east entrance with Jan on your back

DANNY: Is he taking the piss?

PHIL: the weight of the two of you combined should equal that of a fat postman with bad teeth, you make you way into the woods, do not put her down unless it's on concrete or a tree trunk, never when you're walking on mud. You meet Lou near the bridge, you move around a bit, you exit from the South,

MARK: By the Asda.

PHIL: Cathy and Mark you meet them there, but on the way you find a quiet street, you wait until it's just you and a man, you walk ahead of him and when you're far ahead you drop the jumper. The man picks it up, runs after you covering it in DNA and then gives it back, make sure you let him drop it in the bag, say you're taking it to a charity shop. Take it to the south entrance, tear it a little, chuck it in a hedge, all go home and wait a day or two until Adam's declared missing and then John Tate comes forward and says he thinks he saw Adam with a fat man in a uniform by Asda's but he can't be sure, they'll think he's been abducted, they'll be inquiries, police, mourning a service and if everyone keeps their mouths shut we should be fine.

Any questions?

They stare at him open mouthed.

He bends down. Picks up his Coke.

Starts to drink his Coke.

*   *   *

A Field. LEAH and PHIL sitting.

Pause.

LEAH: Apparently bonobos are our nearest relative. For years people thought they were chimpanzees, but they're not, they are completely different. Chimps are evil. They murder each other, did you know that? They kill and sometimes torture each other to find a better position within the social structure. A chimp'll just find itself on the outside of a group and before he knows what's happening it's being hounded to death by the others, sometimes for months. For years we've thought that chimps were our closest living relative, but now they saying it's the bonobos. Bonobos are the complete opposite of chimps. When a stranger bonobo approaches the pack, the other bonobos all come out and go 'Hello, mate. What you doing round here? Come and meet the family, we can eat some ants.' And if a bonobo damages its hand, whereas the chimps'll probably cast it out or bite its hand off, the bonobos will come over and look after it, and they'll all look sad because there's a bonobo feeling pain. I saw it on a program. Such sadness in those intelligent eyes. Empathy. That's what bonobos have. Amazing really, I mean they're exactly like chimps, but the tiniest change in their DNA… The woman was saying that if we'd discovered bonobos before chimps our understanding of ourselves would be very different.

Pause. PHIL pulls out a bag of crisps.

You don't care, do you. I could be talking Chinese for all you care. How do you do it? You're amazing. You're unreal. I sometimes think you're not human. I sometimes think I wonder what you would do if I killed myself, right here in front of you. What would you do? What would you do, Phil?

No answer.

Phil, what would you do? Phil?

Still no answer.

Suddenly she grabs her throat.

I'm gonna do it!

She squeezes.

I mean it! I'm gonna do it…

No answer. She strangles herself, her face turning red.

She falls to her knees with the exertion.

PHIL looks on.

She is in considerable pain. Grits her teeth and squeezes.

She strangles until she is lying prone on the floor.

(Gasping…) Phil! This is it…

She stops.

Lies there, panting.

PHIL opens his crisps and begins to eat them.

LEAH gets up, sits next to PHIL.

PHIL eats on.

Course, they shag a lot. Bonobos. Always at it. Sex mad. Sex, sex, sex, sex, sex, sex, sex, sex, sex, constant sex, randy, in the bonobo world having it off is like saying I like your shoes. Partner swapping, men and women, women and men, women and women, men on men, fathers, mothers, oral, group masturbation, the lot. It was like an orgy, when bonobos get going. It was fairly disgusting, actually.

Pause.

But that's bonobos for you.

Pause.

We're in trouble now.

We're in trouble now, Phil. Don't know how this'll pan out.

Trouble now.

Two

A Street. JAN and MARK.

Pause.

JAN: What?

MARK: He's not going.

JAN: What do you mean he's not going?

MARK: He's not going.

JAN: He's not going?

MARK: Yes.

JAN: That's what he said?

MARK: Yes.

JAN: He said he's not going?

MARK: Yeah, he said he's not, he's not…

JAN: What?

MARK: Going.

Beat.

JAN: Is he off his head?

MARK: I know.

JAN: Is he insane?

MARK: I know.

JAN: Is he joking?

MARK: I know, I know.

JAN: No, that's a question.

MARK: He's not joking, he's not going, he's said he's not going, I said you've gotta go, he said he's not going, 'I'm not going' he said.

JAN: That's what he said?

MARK: That's what he said, I'm saying that's what he said.

JAN: Shit.

MARK: Exactly.

Beat.

JAN: What are we going to do?

*   *   *

A Field. PHIL and LEAH, PHIL slowly eating a pack of Starburst. LEAH has a Tupperware container on her lap.

LEAH: Are you happy?

No, don't answer that, Jesus, sorry, what's wrong with me, sorry –

Are you?

No, I'm just wondering. I mean what is happy, what's happy all about, who says you're supposed to be happy, like we're all supposed to be happy, happy is our natural, and any deviation from that state is seen as a failure, which in itself makes you more unhappy so you have to pretend to be even happier which doesn't work because people can see that you're pretending which makes them awkward and you can see that they can see that you're pretending to be happy and their awkwardness is making you even more unhappy so you have to pretend to be even happier, it's a nightmare. It's like nuclear waste or global warming.

Beat.

Isn't it Phil? Phil? Isn't it, like nuclear…

PHIL doesn't answer.

Yeah, you know, you know it is, you know more than
I do, I can't tell you any, you know. People getting all
upset about polluting the natural order? When this planet
is churning molten lava with a thin layer of crust on
top with a few kilometres of atmosphere clinging to it?
I mean, please, don't gimme all that, carbon dioxide?
Carbon dioxide, Phil? And look at the rest of the universe,
Venus, Phil, there's a, look at Venus, what about Venus,
hot enough to melt lead or Titan with oceans of liquid
nitrogen, I mean stars, Phil, a billion nuclear reactions a
second, I mean to be honest it's all either red hot or ice
cold, so, so, so… No. It's life that upsets the natural order.
It's us that's the anomaly.

But that's the beauty, isn't it Phil. I couldn't say this to
anyone else they'd say 'That's a pretty bloody grim view
of the world, Leah' but you can see the beauty, which is
why I can talk to you, because you can see the incredibly
precious beauty and fragility of reality, and it's the same for
happiness, you can apply the same theory to happiness, so
don't start Phil, don't come here giving it all the, you know,
all the, all the…

Beat.

Can you remember the happiest moment in your life?

Beat. PHIL eats another Toffo.

I know mine. I know my happiest moment. Week last
Tuesday. That sunset. You remember that sunset? Do you?
You don't do you. Oh my God, you don't.

He says nothing.

She opens the Tupperware container.

Shows it to PHIL.

31

It's Jerry. I killed him. I took him out of his cage, I put the point of a screwdriver on his head and I hit it with a hammer. Why do you think I did that?

PHIL shrugs.

No. No, me neither.

She closes the lid.

Everything's much better, though. I mean really, it is. Everyone's working together. They're a lot happier. Remember last month, Dan threatened to kill Cathy? well yesterday I saw him showing her his phone, like they were old friends. Last week Richard invited Mark to his party, bring a friend, anyone you like, can you believe that? Richard and Mark? Yep. Everyone's happier. It's pouring into the school, grief, grief is making them happy.

They say John Tate's lost it though, won't come out of his room. Bit odd. Maybe that's what's making people happier. Maybe it's just having something to work towards. Together. Do you think that's what it is. Are we really that simple?

Where will it stop? Only been four days but everything's changed

Pause.

Adam's parents were on the telly again last night.

PHIL looks up.

Yeah. Another appeal.

To the fat postman with bad teeth.

What have we done, Phil?

MARK and JAN enter.

JAN: We need to talk.

*   *   *

A Wood. PHIL and LEAH, LOU and DANNY. PHIL has a muffin.

Pause.

LEAH: What?

DANNY: They've found...

They...

Well they've found –

LOU: The man.

DANNY: Yeah, they've found the man.

LEAH: They've found the man?

DANNY: Yeah.

LEAH: They've found the man?

DANNY: Yes.

LEAH: Oh my god.

LOU: Exactly.

LEAH: Oh my god.

LOU: That's what we thought, we thought that, didn't we, Danny.

DANNY: Yeah, we did.

LEAH: Are you sure? I mean are you...

DANNY: Definitely. He's in custody now. They're questioning him.

LEAH: But how, I mean who, how, who, who is, who is, how?

LOU: Dunno.

LEAH: Who is he?

LOU: He's the man who kidnapped Adam.

LEAH: Right. No.

LOU: Yes.

LEAH: No.

DANNY: Yes.

LEAH: No, no, yeah, no, actually, because that man, the man who, he doesn't actually, I mean I'm not being fussy or anything, but the man who kidnapped Adam doesn't actually exist, does he. Well does he?

LOU: No. But they've got him.

DANNY: I heard his teeth are awful.

LEAH: You know, I mean he doesn't, he doesn't… Phil? Any… any thoughts? Any words, any comments, any…ideas, any, any, any…thing? At all?

I mean this is, this is, isn't it, this is, is it?

Shit. Oh shit.

DANNY: He answers the description. Fat postman, thinning hair, his teeth are terrible, apparently.

LEAH: But that's just

LOU: Yeah. That's what we thought.

LEAH: we just, didn't we, Phil, we just, we just, I mean you just…

DANNY: What are we gonna do?

LOU: We're screwed.

LEAH: We're not…

LOU: We're –

LEAH: No, no, sorry, no we're not, are we Phil, I mean we're, no we're alright.

DANNY: They're looking for Brian.

LEAH: Why?

DANNY: Because he can identify him.

LEAH: No he can't.

LOU: Because he saw him in the woods.

LEAH: He didn't

LOU: He did, he –

LEAH: No he didn't because that wasn't the man in the woods because there wasn't a man in the woods.

Where's Brian?

DANNY: Hiding. Dan and Mark have gone to find him.

LOU: He's shitting it.

LEAH: I mean what, they just picked this bloke up, they just saw him and said 'You look dodgy, you're a murderer because you've got a postman's uniform'?

DANNY: Well, there's the teeth as well.

LEAH: You can't go to prison for bad teeth.

LOU: What if he goes to prison?

LEAH: He won't go to prison.

LOU: You just said –

LEAH: He won't get done for it because he hasn't…

DANNY: This sort of stuff sticks, you know.

LEAH: Look, everyone, everyone calm, okay. Isn't that right, Phil. Phil, isn't that, I mean things are, everything is, well, better and isn't everyone more, you know, and cheerful and stuff, so lets, please, let's –

DANNY: How am I gonna get references?

LOU: We are completely –

LEAH: We are not –

DANNY: You need three references for dental college, how am I gonna get references?

RICHARD enters with CATHY.

RICHARD: We just came from the police station. It's full of reporters.

CATHY: It was great.

RICHARD: It was shit. Phil, have you heard?

LEAH: We heard.

CATHY: They wanted to interview me.

RICHARD: You've heard? You know?

CATHY: Didn't have time, but I'm gonna go back

RICHARD: So you know they've caught him?

CATHY: get on the telly

LEAH: How can they have caught someone who doesn't exist?

RICHARD: I don't know, Leah.

LEAH: Because that's impossible.

RICHARD: Why don't you tell them that? Why don't you pop down the station and say 'excuse me, but that fat postman with the bad teeth doesn't actually exist, so why don't you let him go?'

LEAH: Sarcasm, that's the lowest.

CATHY: they might even give me money for it, do you think I should ask for money?

LOU: He's gonna go to prison.

LEAH: Lou, they are not going to send him to prison because he answers a description they need more than that, they need fibres, they need samples, they need evidence.

RICHARD: DNA evidence.

LEAH: Exactly, they need DNA –

RICHARD: No, they've got DNA evidence.

Beat.

LEAH: What?

RICHARD: He answers the description, but they've got DNA evidence linking him to the crime.

LEAH: DN… What are you talking about?

RICHARD: We spoke to a reporter. They matched up the DNA evidence they found on the jumper to a police database and they came up with this man, this man who answers the description perfectly.

LEAH: That's impossible.

RICHARD: Well it's what happened.

LEAH: No, because, we made that description up and they got DNA from a random –

Beat. She turns to CATHY.

Cathy?

Pause. They all stare at CATHY.

CATHY: You told us to get DNA evidence. We got DNA evidence. We did what you said.

LEAH: Right.

Okay.

Hang on.

Where did you get the DNA evidence?

CATHY: From a man, like you said.

Beat.

A man down at the sorting office.

They stare at her.

LEAH: What?

CATHY: Well, we thought, you know, I mean you'd given a description so we thought, well, I thought, you know, show initiative, we'll look for a fat balding postman with bad teeth.

They stare at her.

There were quite a few.

DANNY: Oh my god.

CATHY: What?

LOU: Oh my god.

CATHY: We showed…initiative, we –

LEAH: And who asked you to do that?

CATHY: Richard, we showed initiative.

RICHARD: That is the most stupid –

DANNY: Oh, Jesus.

CATHY: Why?

LEAH: Why? Because there is now a man in prison who is linked to a non-existent crime, answering a description that Brian gave.

LOU: Oh, Jesus Christ.

CATHY: But isn't that…

LEAH: No, Cathy, it is not what we wanted.

RICHARD: What we wanted was to cover up what had happened, not to frame someone else.

LOU: We're screwed.

LEAH: Yes. We might actually be… This is a nightmare.

DANNY: We can't let them think it's him. I mean, I really can't be mixed up in something like that, it wouldn't be right.

LOU: What if he goes to prison?

RICHARD: What if we go to prison?

LEAH: Yes, I think now, we might just actually be a little bit, well, screwed.

JAN and MARK enter with BRIAN. BRIAN is crying.

BRIAN: I'm not going in.

RICHARD: You dick, Mark.

MARK: It was her idea!

LOU: Mark, you dick.

BRIAN: I'm not going to the police station.

JAN: He has to. They're looking for him.

BRIAN: I can't go in. It was bad enough talking to them before, saying what I said, but I can't do it again.

JAN: They're searching everywhere for him. They want him to identify the man.

BRIAN: I can't identify him, I can't go in there, don't make me go in there, I'm not going in there.

DANNY: This is terrible.

BRIAN: I can't face it. They look at me. They look at me like I'm lying and it makes me cry. I can't stand the way they look at me. And then, because I cry, they think I'm telling the truth, but I'm crying because I'm lying and I feel terrible inside.

LOU: We're going to have to tell them.

LEAH: Maybe we could do nothing?

DANNY: We can't do nothing, they want Brian.

BRIAN: I'm not going in.

LEAH: Phil?

No answer.

Phil?

Pause. PHIL walks over to BRIAN and lays a hand on his shoulder.

PHIL: This is a bad situation. We didn't want this situation. But we've got this situation. It wasn't supposed to be like this. But it is like this.

Beat.

You're going in.

BRIAN: No.

PHIL: Yes.

BRIAN: No, Phil –

PHIL: Yes, yes, shhhh, yes. Sorry. You have to go in. Or we'll take you up the grille.

Pause.

We'll throw you in.

RICHARD: Er, Phil.

DANNY: Is he serious?

LEAH: He's always serious.

PHIL: We'll take you up the grille now. We'll get you by the arms. By the legs. And we'll swing you onto the grille. We'll throw rocks at you until you drop through. You'll drop through. You'll fall into the cold. Into the dark. You'll land on Adam's corpse and you'll rot together.

Beat.

We're in trouble now. We need your help. If you don't help us we'll kill you. Are you going to help us?

Pause.

BRIAN nods.

Okay. You go in there. Richard'll take you

RICHARD: Not me again.

PHIL: Richard'll take you. You take a look at that man and you say it's him. You say it's the man in the woods. That's what you do. Okay?

Slowly, BRIAN nods.

Everyone else stays calm. Keep your mouths shut. Tell no one or we'll all go to prison. Just get on with things.

He starts to eat his pie. They stare at him.

*   *   *

A Field. PHIL and LEAH, PHIL picking his teeth.

Silence.

Suddenly LEAH jumps up, shocked.

LEAH: Woah! Woah, woah, woah…

No reaction from PHIL.

I just had déjà vu, but really strong, I just…

and you were…

I was…

I mean we were just here and, and…

I was sitting like that and…

Woah. I've been here before, Phil. Phil?

PHIL carries on picking his teeth.

LEAH watches, then explodes.

That's exactly what you did when I said Phil! I knew you were going to do that, I said Phil and you picked your teeth, Phil, you just carried on picking your teeth!

Oh my god. This might be the real thing. Maybe I have been here before. Maybe this has all happened before. Phil? Do you think this has happened before? I know what you're gonna do next. I can see, I know, I know, you're gonna…you're gonna…you're gonna…do nothing!

PHIL does nothing.

Yes! Yes, yes, yes, yes, yes! You see? This is amazing, this is, the world has just changed, reality is not what we think, Phil maybe, this isn't real, maybe we're caught in some sort of…hang on, hang on, a bird is going to…a starling, a starling is going to land by that stone…now!

Nothing happens.

Now!

Still nothing happens.

Any minute…now!

Again, nothing happens.

LEAH sags. She sits back with PHIL.

Look at that sky.

Have you ever seen a sky like that? I've never seen a sky quite like that. Strange time we've been born in. No other time quite like this one.

Pause.

Do you think it's possible to change things? I know, I know, but I feel like this time… I dunno, this time… I feel like this is an important time. Do you think people always feel like that? D'you think we're doomed to behave like people before us did?

Phil?

No answer.

Phil?

Phil?

Phil?

Phil?

Phil?

Phil?

Phil?

Phil?

Phil?

Pause.

PHIL!

Slowly PHIL turns to her.

If you change one thing you can change the world. Do you believe that?

PHIL: No.

LEAH: Right.

Well I do.

I do, Phil.

Beat.

Phil?

Three

A Street. JAN and MARK.

JAN: Okay. Okay. Okay.

> *Beat.*

> Okay.

> No.

MARK: Yes.

JAN: No, no

MARK: yes

JAN: no. No way, that's

MARK: I know

JAN: that's

MARK: I know, I know

JAN: And are you…is this…

> I mean are you…there's no mistake or…

MARK: No.

JAN: Because this is

MARK: That's what I'm saying

JAN: this is really

MARK: Yeah, yes, yeah.

JAN: really, really

MARK: Exactly.

JAN: Are you sure?

MARK: Yes.

JAN: Where?

MARK: In the woods.

JAN: In the woods?

MARK: In the woods, Cathy found him in the woods

JAN: Cathy?

MARK: Yes.

JAN: Cathy found him...?

MARK: Yes, she

JAN: in the woods?

MARK: Yes.

Beat.

JAN: Cathy found him in the woods?

MARK: Yes.

JAN: Oh.

MARK: I know.

JAN: I don't…

MARK: I know, I know.

JAN: This is…

MARK: Yeah.

JAN: Does anyone know?

MARK: You and me. And Cathy. For the moment.

JAN: Right.

Right.

Pause.

Right.

*   *   *

A Field. PHIL sits with a bag.

Takes out a paper plate.

Places a waffle on it.

Takes out a pack of butter and a jar of jam.

Takes out a knife.

LEAH turns up. She is carrying a suitcase.

He stares at her.

LEAH: I'm going. I'm out of here, I'm gone, I'm, I'm, this is it. I'm running away, Phil.

PHIL says nothing.

Where'm I going? I dunno. Wherever the universe decides that I should be. It's a big world, Phil, a lot bigger than you, it's a lot bigger than you and me, a lot bigger than all this, these people, sitting here, a lot bigger, a lot lot bigger.

Pause. PHIL starts to butter his waffle.

Don't. No words. There's no point, so… What's the point? 'Why are you going, is it me, is it us, is it what we've done, is it what we're becoming, why Leah, why, is it me, is it the impossibility of ever saying exactly what you mean?' There's no point, Phil. So don't even try. I'm outta here. I'm gone. I am part of history, I'm on a jet-plane, I'm moving, I'm discovering, I'm, I'm, sayonara baby, sayonara Phil and hello discovery and, yeah don't try and stop me, because, because, exit stage left Leah, right now. Right now.

PHIL stops buttering the waffle.

Opens the jam.

Starts putting a thin layer of jam on the waffle.

Right now. Right now, Phil, right, bloody… I mean it! I really, really…

Pause. PHIL continues with his waffle.

You're not going to stop me, are you. You're not even thinking of stopping me. You're not even thinking of thinking of stopping me. The only thing in you brain at the moment is that waffle. Your brain is entirely waffle, single-mindedly waffle and maybe a bit of jam, I don't know how you do it. I admire you so much.

PHIL decides that the waffle needs more jam.

LEAH sags. She drops her suitcase and sits with PHIL.

Did you see Jan at Adam's memorial? Floods of tears. It was wonderful, everyone felt wonderful, I felt terrible of course, but everyone felt wonderful. It's incredible. The change. This place. You're a miracle worker. Everyone's happy. You know that? You notice that? Cathy was on the telly. Used that clip on every channel. She's like a celebrity, there are second years asking for her autograph. Suddenly Adam's everyone's best friend. Richard's named his dog Adam. Mark's mum says if her baby's a boy she's going to call him Adam. Funny thing is they're all actually behaving better as well. I saw Jan helping a first year find the gym. Mark's been doing charity work, for Christ's sake. Maybe being seen as heroes is making them behave like heroes

PHIL considers his waffle. Decides it needs more jam.

Yeah, everyone happy. Well it's not all roses, you know. Brian's on medication. Did you know that? Phil? Did you know that they've put Brian on medication?

No answer.

Yep, Brian's off his head, John Tate hasn't been seen in weeks, and the postman's facing the rest of his life in prison, but, you know, omelettes and eggs, as long as you've your waffle, who cares.

How do you feel?

PHIL turns to her.

Considers.

For a long time.

Opens his mouth to answer.

Stops.

Shrugs and goes back to his waffle.

LEAH stares at him.

LEAH: I admire you so much.

The waffle is ready. PHIL looks pleased.

JAN and MARK enter.

JAN: You better come with us.

MARK: You really better come with us.

LEAH: What is it?

Beat.

JAN: You really, really better come with us.

LEAH goes with JAN and MARK.

PHIL looks at his waffle, looks after JAN, MARK and LEAH, then back at the waffle. Irritated he puts it carefully away.

* * *

48

A Wood. CATHY, BRIAN, LEAH, MARK, LOU and JAN.

They stand around a boy who looks like a tramp. His clothes are torn and dirty and his hair is matted with dried blood from an old gash on his forehead that has not been cleaned up. He stands there, twitchily, staring at them as though they were Aliens and it looks as though he might run off at any moment.

Finally PHIL speaks.

PHIL: Hello Adam.

ADAM: Alright.

Pause.

CATHY: We found him up there, up the hill

BRIAN: I found him

CATHY: living in a hedge

BRIAN: a hedge, I found him, I found him, I found Adam living in a hedge, I found him

CATHY: It's like this hedge complex he's made, you have to crawl to get in

BRIAN: I crawled, I love crawling, I love crawling, Leah

CATHY: Like a warren in this hedge and he's dragged bits of cardboard and rags to make it better, more waterproof

BRIAN: I loved it, Leah, it was like a hideout.

CATHY: He's been living in there.

BRIAN: Living, she was shouting at me to get off the ground, but I love the ground, don't you like the ground?

CATHY: He was hiding away at the back.

BRIAN: D'you ever feel like the trees are watching you?

CATHY: Terrified.

ADAM: No I wasn't.

BRIAN: D'you ever want to rub your face against the earth?

JAN: No.

BRIAN: He wouldn't speak to us. I don't think he knew his name.

ADAM: Adam, my name's, I've got a name, it's…

BRIAN: Shall we do that? Shall we rub our faces against the earth? What do you think, shall we rub our faces against the earth?

CATHY: I think his head's hurt.

MARK: Who, Brian's or Adam's?

BRIAN: Don't they eat earth somewhere? Shall we eat the earth? I wonder what earth tastes like, what do you think it, do you think it tastes earthy, or, or…

He bends down to eat a handful of earth.

CATHY: I think he's been up there for weeks. Hiding.

I don't think he's very well.

BRIAN: *(Spitting the earth out.)* That's disgusting!

He suddenly starts giggling as he scrapes the earth from his mouth.

CATHY: I dunno how he's survived, what he's eaten.

BRIAN: *(Like it's hilarious.)* He's probably been eating earth!

He bursts into laughter.

CATHY: It took me half an hour to get him to come out.

BRIAN: D'you feel how wonderful this day is?

CATHY: I used violence.

BRIAN: She did.

CATHY: I threatened to gouge one of his eyes out.

BRIAN: She was gonna do it. She loves violence now. Can you feel the day licking our skin?

CATHY: He's a mess.

MARK: Which one?

BRIAN: Shall we hold hands? Come on, let's hold, let's hold, let's hold hands, come on, let's –

Suddenly CATHY slaps him.

For a second he looks as if he might cry, but instead he just giggles.

LEAH: Okay. Right. Okay.

Adam.

ADAM: Huh?

LEAH: Hello, Adam. How are you?

ADAM: ...

LEAH: Yeah. Great. Phil?

PHIL says nothing.

Because this is a bit...isn't it. I mean this is really, talk about a bolt from the, yeah, shit. No, not shit, I mean it's good

LOU: Good?

LEAH: it's, yeah, yes it's

JAN: How is it good?

LEAH: it's, it's good, Adam, that found, but I mean yes, it does make things a bit

LOU: Screwed?

LEAH: tricky, no, not...don't say

LOU: We are absolutely –

JAN: What are we gonna do?

LEAH: Don't panic.

MARK: What are we gonna do?

LEAH: I said don't panic.

MARK: We're not panicking.

LEAH: Good, because that's the one thing that's... So. Adam.
How's...how's...how's things?

ADAM: I know my name.

LEAH: Yes you do.

ADAM: Adam, it's Adam, my name's Adam.

LEAH: Good. Well that's...

BRIAN starts giggling.

No, no, no Brian, that's, that's not gonna, so shut up.
Please.

CATHY: What are we going to do?

LEAH: Phil?

What are we gonna...?

Phil?

Phil?

Say something Phil!

Pause. But PHIL says nothing.

LEAH: What happened.

ADAM doesn't answer.

LEAH goes to him.

What happened?

ADAM: I…

I was in a

dark…

Beat.

walking, crawling in this dark, when you're moving but
with you hands and knees, crawl, crawling in this

dark

place and I don't remember

things

I fell, I falled into, I fell onto this…

wake, woke, wake up, I woke up with liquid on my head,
leaves, dead and rotting, I remember leaves, but just dark
maybe a light high, high, high, high, high…

above and, I drank the liquid it was blood, there was, it
was mine, so I, it's not wrong because it was my

crawling for a long time, I thought, but that was hard to
tell, tunnels, scared, I was, I felt like the dark was my fear,
do you know what I mean? I was wrapped in it. Like a soft
blanket.

And then I came out.

I saw this

light, this daylight light, I saw this light and went that way,
towards, and I thought I died because that's what people

go to the light, you

and there was such a pain in my

I thought the light would make it go, but it didn't because
the

light was…this.

Beat.

I was confused.

Beat.

Outside. I was sad, crushed.

Came outside.

I couldn't remember things.

I couldn't remember anything.

I was new.

A new

a new

a new me. And I felt

happy.

It hurt to laugh. But I laughed.

Beat.

Then night came and then I was

panicked, because, again dark, I panicked again

I ran

scratching there was lots of, scratching my skin

and I found my place where I live, and that's where I live now, I live there.

And I do know my name so you can shut, you can...

I live there. It's

mine, I

live

there.

Adam.

I'm not coming back.

Beat.

It's Adam.

LEAH: How've you been living?

ADAM: In the hedge.

LEAH: No, how?

What have you been eating?

ADAM: You can eat anything. I eat things.

Nothing dead, I don't

insects, grass, leaves, all good, but nothing, I caught
a rabbit once and ate that, it's fur was soft, warm, but
nothing, I found a dead bird and ate some of that but it
made me sick so nothing, nothing dead, that's the rule,
nothing

Beat.

What?

JAN: Jesus Christ.

MARK: He's lost it.

JAN: He's off his –

LEAH: Okay. Now things are strange. Things are really, really
strange, Phil. I mean with the greatest of respect, Adam,
you are supposed to be dead.

ADAM: Dead?

LEAH: And I mean, there's been a service, there's been
appeals, there's been weeping... They're naming the
science lab after him, for god's sake.

ADAM: I'm...dead?

BRIAN starts giggling.

CATHY: Shut up.

ADAM: Am I dead?

LEAH: I mean now we really have, I don't know how we're
   gonna get out of this one because now we really have

ADAM: I thought I was dead.

LOU: You're not dead.

CATHY: (*To BRIAN.*) If you don't shut up you'll be dead.

BRIAN: I love this! This is great! Mates!

JAN: What are we going to do?

MARK: Yeah, what are we going to do?

LEAH: We're gonna, right, we're gonna... What are we
   gonna do?

PHIL: Adam?

ADAM: Yes?

PHIL: Do you want to come back?

ADAM: What?

PHIL: With us.

ADAM: I

PHIL: Or do you want to stay? Are you happy? Here?

LEAH: Phil –

PHIL: Shut up. Do you want to stay?

   Pause. ADAM thinks. Looks at PHIL.

   PHIL smiles, kindly. Nods.

   Brian? Take Adam back to his hedge. Then come back
   to us.

BRIAN: This is great!

BRIAN takes ADAM off. They all stare at PHIL.

LEAH: What's going on?

PHIL: *(To MARK and JAN.)* Go back home. Don't say anything to anybody about this. You too, Lou.

LEAH: Phil…?

JAN: Are we going to be in trouble.

PHIL: If you go now and you say nothing to no one about this, you won't be in trouble.

She thinks. Nods to MARK. They go.

LOU stands there, unsure.

LOU: What about…

What about Cathy?

PHIL goes to her. Places a hand on her shoulder, smiles, warm, reassuring.

PHIL: Everything is going to be fine.

Beat. She goes off after JAN and MARK.

LEAH: Phil, what are you doing?

What? But he's…

Beat.

Phil, he's off his head. He's injured, he's been living off insects for weeks, he's insane Phil, he needs help.

PHIL: He's happy.

LEAH: He's not happy, he's mad.

PHIL: He doesn't want to come back.

LEAH: Because he's mad! We can't leave him here, I mean that's not, are you serious? Are you seriously –

Alright, yes, there'll be –

Phil, this is insane. I mean I've never, but this, because, alright, whatever, but this is actually insane. We can't just leave him up here.

PHIL: I'm in charge. Everyone is happier. What's more important; one person or everyone?

She stares at him.

LEAH: It's Adam, Phil, Adam! We used to go to his birthday parties, he used to have that cheap ice cream and we used to take the piss, remember?

PHIL: If he comes back our lives are ruined. He can't come back, Cathy.

LEAH: Oh, great, now you're talking to Cathy, like, I'm not, I'm not, because you don't like what I say and now it's Cathy, you sit there and you say nothing for years and suddenly now you chatting with Cathy.

PHIL: Cathy?

LEAH: Let's, come on, let's, it won't be that bad, it'll be, we can explain, we can talk. We can go through the whole thing and make them understand –

PHIL: *(To CATHY.)* Do you understand?

LEAH: Understand what?

CATHY: Yeah. I do.

LEAH: Oh great, now you're at it.

BRIAN comes back, giggling.

(Pointing at BRIAN.) I mean I might as well talk to him for all the sense I'm getting. Phil, we can't do this, I mean what if he comes down next week, next year, in ten years, even?

PHIL: Take Brian.

CATHY: Okay.

BRIAN: We going somewhere?

LEAH: No, no, wait, you can't, no, this is… Cathy?

PHIL: Make a game of it.

BRIAN: We gonna play a game?

PHIL: You and Cathy are going to play a game. With Adam

BRIAN: Brilliant!

CATHY: How?

LEAH: How what? What are you, will you please talk to me as if

PHIL: Brian?

BRIAN: Who?

PHIL: Come here.

BRIAN goes to PHIL.

PHIL: I'm gonna do an experiment with this plastic bag. I want you to stay still while I do this experiment.

BRIAN: I love experiments! Will there be fire?

PHIL: *(Emptying his carrier bag.)* No. No fire.

Stay still.

PHIL places the bag over BRIAN's head.

BRIAN: It's all gone dark.

He pulls the handles back around his neck and to opposite corners, making it airtight.

BRIAN is giggling inside, looking around and breathing the plastic in and out of his mouth.

Bit stuffy.

PHIL looks to CATHY. She nods.

This is great!

LEAH: Phi… Phil?

PHIL takes the bag off.

BRIAN: That was great!

PHIL: You just do what Cathy says.

BRIAN: I am brilliant at doing what people say.

LEAH: No! Stop, don't, don't, Phil, don't, what are you doing, what are you…

PHIL: He's dead. Everyone thinks he's dead. What difference will it make?

She stares at him.

LEAH: But he's not dead. He's alive.

CATHY: Come on Brian.

BRIAN: This is brilliant.

LEAH: No, Cathy, don't, stop, Cathy…?

But she goes, taking BRIAN with her. LEAH turns to PHIL.

Phil?

Phil?

Please!

Please, Phil!

But PHIL just walks away.

*   *   *

A Field. PHIL and LEAH, sitting.

Complete silence.

PHIL takes out a pack of Starburst.

Opens.

Has one.

Chews. Thinks.

He offers one to LEAH.

She takes it.

She begins to quietly cry.

Crying, she puts the sweet in her mouth and begins to chew.

PHIL puts his arm around her.

Suddenly she stops chewing and spits the sweet out.

Gets up, stares at PHIL.

Storms off.

PHIL: Leah?

Leah?

Four

A Street. JAN and MARK.

JAN: Gone?

MARK: Yeah.

JAN: Gone?

MARK: Yeah.

JAN: What, she's gone?

MARK: Yes.

Beat.

JAN: When?

MARK: Last week.

JAN: Where?

MARK: Dunno. No one knows.

JAN: No one knows?

MARK: Well, not no one, I mean someone must, but no one I know knows.

JAN: I mean she must've gone somewhere.

MARK: Moved schools. That's what people are saying.

JAN: Moved schools?

MARK: Yeah.

JAN: Just like that?

MARK: Just like that.

JAN: Without saying anything?

MARK: Without saying a thing

Pause.

JAN: Oh.

MARK: Yeah.

JAN: Oh.

MARK: Yeah.

JAN: Oh.

MARK: I know.

JAN: Does Phil know?

*   *   *

A Field. RICHARD sits with PHIL.

PHIL is not eating. He stares into the distance.

Silence.

Suddenly RICHARD gets up.

RICHARD: Phil, Phil, watch this! Phil, watch me, watch me, Phil!

He walks on his hands.

See? See what I'm doing? Can you see, Phil?

He collapses. PHIL doesn't even look at him.

RICHARD gets up, brushes himself down, and sits with PHIL.

Silence.

When are you going to come back?

PHIL shrugs.

Come on, Phil. Come back to us. What do you want to sit up here for? In this field? Don't you get bored? Don't you get bored sitting here, everyday, doing nothing?

No answer.

Everyone's asking after you. You know that? Everyone's saying 'where's Phil?' 'what's Phil up to?' 'when's Phil going to come down from that stupid field?' 'wasn't it good when Phil was running the show?' What do you think about that? What do you think about everyone asking after you?

No answer.

Aren't you interested? Aren't you interested in what's going on?

No answer.

John Tate's found god. Yeah, Yeah I know. He's joined the Jesus Army, he runs round the shopping centre singing and trying to give people leaflets. Danny's doing work experience at a dentist's. He hates it. Can't stand the cavities, he says when they open their mouths sometimes it feels like you're going to fall in.

Pause.

Brian's on stronger and stronger medication. They caught him staring at a wall and drooling last week. It's either drooling or giggling. Keeps talking about earth. I think they're going to section him. Cathy doesn't care. She's too busy running things. You wouldn't believe how thing's have got, Phil. She's insane. She cut a first year's finger off, that's what they say anyway.

Doesn't that bother you? Aren't you even bothered?

No answer.

Lou's her best friend, now. Dangerous game. I feel sorry for Lou. And Jan and Mark have taken up shoplifting, they're really good at it, get you anything you want.

Phil?

Phil!

He shakes PHIL by the shoulders. Slowly PHIL looks at him.

You can't stay here forever. When are you going to come down?

PHIL says nothing. RICHARD lets go.

PHIL goes back to staring at nothing.

Pause.

Nice up here.

As I was coming up here there was this big wind of fluff. You know, this big wind of fluff, like dandelions, but smaller, and tons of them, like fluffs of wool or cotton, it was really weird, I mean it just came out of nowhere, this big wind of fluff, and for a minute I thought I was in a cloud, Phil. Imagine that. Imagine being inside a cloud, but with space inside it as well, for a second, as I was coming up here I felt like I was an alien in a cloud. But really felt it. And in that second, Phil, I knew that there was life on other planets. I knew we weren't alone in the universe, I didn't just think it or feel it, I knew it, I know it, it was as if the universe was suddenly shifting and giving me a glimpse, this vision that could see everything, just for a fraction of a heartbeat of a second. But I couldn't see who they were or what they were doing or how they were living.

How do you think they're living, Phil?

How do you think they're living?

No answer.

There are more stars in the universe that grains of sand on Brighton beach.

Pause.

Come back, Phil.

Phil?

65

No answer. They sit in silence.

End.

NOTES ON DNA

Single and group activity suggestions for teachers and students studying Dennis Kelly's play for GCSE English in order to get inside the play text and gain a thorough understanding of its story, characters, style, structure and themes.

THE STORY

Why do you think Dennis Kelly chose to write this story and have a group of teenage characters tell it?

The story begins immediately after a small group of people have carried out a violent and disturbing act. Explain how the storyteller reveals the details of the unseen act through his characters.

Each character responds to what has happened just before the story begins in a different way – explain how their various types of response illustrate what sort of character they are.

CHARACTERS

Each person in the group should choose a character from *DNA* so that all characters are covered.

Firstly, note down facts about your character according to all the hard evidence you can find in the play text. You should look carefully at what other characters say about your character, as well as the scenes in which your character features.

Secondly, use your imagination to fill in the areas you don't know about your character, with as much detail as you can think of, you should include everything from their family backgrounds to what their favourite music might be. You will find clues in the conversation that Richard and Phil have in the final scene.

Do any characters say the same line more than once? What recurring traits can you discover in the way they behave and react from moment to moment?

What effect do you think this makes the play have on the listener?

Read through scenes three, seven and eleven carefully. These are large group scenes.

Take each scene and work out the status of the characters in the scene from highest to lowest. Note if their status shifts during the scene. Then compare the status of characters and how it changes across all three of these scenes.

STRUCTURE

Grasping an understanding of the sequence of events

The play is divided into fourteen short scenes.

Create a large chart on the wall giving each scene a number from one to fourteen, running left to right. For each scene, list all the characters which appear in each scene. Make a note of who is present at the beginning of the scene, and who arrives into the scene, and who leaves.

Decide what the most crucial action is in each scene, and also the most crucial line of dialogue.

Give each scene a name according to the most important event which happens in it.

You'll notice the play is also divided into four parts. Label the four parts on your chart. Think about why Dennis Kelly decided to segment his play into these four parts. Give each part a title and a summary about what happens in each part.

SETTING

Locations in which the play takes place

On your wall display, colour code each scene with three colours, according to whether it takes place in the Street, the Field or the Wood.

Discuss why certain actions happen in certain places.

Also, discuss the order and frequency that we return to these places.

Now find photos which could be the three locations the play takes place in.

Gather them together and put them on the wall around the chart.

Discuss why Dennis Kelly has chosen these sorts of locations for his story to unfold in.

How do the locations contribute to the effectiveness of the story?

You will have realised that the whole play takes place in outdoor public places – how does this decision affect the telling of the story?

Now find photos of the locations and characters which we don't see during the play, but which are vital in the story.

What is the effect of us not encountering these people, or seeing these places?

STYLE AND LANGUAGE

Some of the characters say a lot and some say very little.

Some characters prefer to speak and some prefer to listen.

Read through the play with everyone taking on the part of one character.

Observe closely the occasions when that character speaks a lot, and when they mainly listen. Discuss how this contributes to our understanding of their character.

Dennis Kelly has made precise choices about the particular words and phrases his characters speak to explain their actions. Analyse the type of speech patterns, descriptive words and phrases your character uses throughout the play.

Write down the most significant lines you think your character has. You should include both questions and statements. Choose lines which reveal something about their instincts, fears, expectations and assumptions. Choose sentences which demonstrate a change in thought. Find phrases which are particularly commanding or decisive, which influence the way the story proceeds.

Explain the different types of language which are used to describe, argue and persuade. Think about where these characters' language comes from: is it a result of their culture, the gang they hang out with, their environment, their family, their race, or their local speech habits?

Leah has some significant speeches in the play. Read through her speeches in isolation from scenes two, four, six, eight and twelve. What she has to say isn't always directly connected to the main strands of the plot. Think about how her descriptions of the other things she talks about creates a suitable universe for this story to exist in. What impact does her discovery and understanding of the world around her have on her reactions to the events of the story? How does this 'close-up' on her consciousness affect our reception of the decisions that her peers make?

THEMES

When you have read the play, and discussed its story and characters, you'll be able to explore the themes the play presents.

What is the overall effect of conveying these themes through a live drama?

What questions and thoughts do you think will buzz around the audience's heads as they leave the theatre?